BIG GUITAR CHORD BOOK

By Richard Moran

6 Strings - Big Guitar Chord Book

Edition I

www.MoranEducation.com/6Strings

ISBN 978-1-4709-2711-0

Introduction

Our Guitar Chord Grids explained

6 Strings employs a unique horizontal grid layout to display our guitar chords. This is a system proven to speed up the learning process, as it is far easier to absorb the information in this format rather than in the vertical format usually employed in guitar books.

The circles shown on our guitar chord diagrams each correspond to a finger on the left hand.

Introduction

For example, to play this chord of C Major, put fingers one two and three in the positions indicated, and either do not play the lowest string, or deaden the string by touching it lightly with either the adjacent third finger, or with the fourth finger.

Next to the grid on the left, you can see how this would actually look on the guitar shown on the right.

An 'X' to the left of a string shows that the string should not be played or strummed, or should be deadened by another finger.

In this book, the top line of the grid or chord diagram always corresponds to the highest sounding string on the guitar. The lowest line corresponds to the lowest sounding (and thickest) string.

Introduction | *More about Chords*

Bar Chords, and chords in higher positions:

8 fr.

Here's an alternative fingering for the chord of C Major. To play the chord, '8 fr.' means you must move your left hand up to the eighth fret of the guitar. You'll notice that there are multiple notes to be played with the first finger. This is called a Bar. Place the first finger flat across all six strings on the eighth fret, and place fingers two three and four as normal to create the chord.

Chords where no fret number is specified always start at the first fret.

Quick tips:

Is your chord not listed in the book? Remember that...

A ♭ can also be written as G#
B ♭ can also be written as A#
C# can also be written as D ♭
E ♭ can also be written as D#
F# can also be written as G ♭

... so if the given chord is D ♭ maj7, substitute C#maj7 instead.. it's actually exactly the same chord!

Introduction

Other chord naming conventions:

There are multiple naming conventions for chords. We've used the most popular versions in our book. In case you encounter any other ways of writing these chords, we've put together a quick guide below...

In these examples, we've substituted 'X' for the first letter of the chord.

Major Chords - These are sometimes written as XMaj, or XM. In this book, we use just 'X'

Minor Chords - Are sometimes written as Xmin or Xmi. We use Xm.

Chords with a '-' sign in them are also sometimes written with a ' ♭ ' instead

Chords with a '+' sign in them are also sometimes written with a '#' instead

Diminished Seventh Chords are shown as a 'X°'. They can also be written as X°7, Xdim7, X-7, and Xdim

Suspended Chords - 'sus' chords can also be written as 'sus4'

'7sus', 'sus7', and '7sus4' are all exactly the same.

Augmented chords can be written as '+', '#5', '+5', or 'aug'

Major Sixth chords can be written as '6', 'Maj6, or 'M6'

Major Sixth add Nine can be written as '6/9, 6(add9'), 'Maj6(add9)', or 'M6(add9)'

'X7' is sometimes written as 'X Dom 7'

Chords

A♭ is also known as G#

A♭

A♭ (alternate)

A♭ (alternate)

A♭7

A♭7 (alternate)

A♭7 (alternate)

A♭m

A♭m (alternate)

A♭m (alternate)

A♭

A♭ m7

A♭ m7 (alternate)

A♭ m7 (alternate)

A♭ maj7

A♭ maj7 (alternate)

A♭ maj7 (alternate)

A♭ maj7 ♭ 5

A♭ 2

A♭ sus2

A♭ sus4

A♭ 7sus4

A♭ 6

Chords

Continued

A♭ m6

A♭ 9

A♭ m9

A♭ maj9

A♭ add9

A♭ add9(no3)

A♭ 6/9

A♭ 7+9

A♭ 7−9

A♭

A ♭ aug

A ♭ +5

A ♭ 7+5

A ♭ dim

A ♭ −5

A ♭ 7−5

A ♭ 9−5

A ♭ 11

A ♭ 13

A ♭ 3
Power Chord

A ♭ 5
Power Chord

A ♭ °
Power Chord

©2011 Moran Education http://www.MoranEducation.com/6Strings

A ♭

A Chords

A A (alternate) A (alternate)

A7 A7 (alternate) A7 (alternate)

Am Am (alternate) Am (alternate)

Big Guitar Chord Book
©2011 Moran Education http://www.MoranEducation.com/6Strings

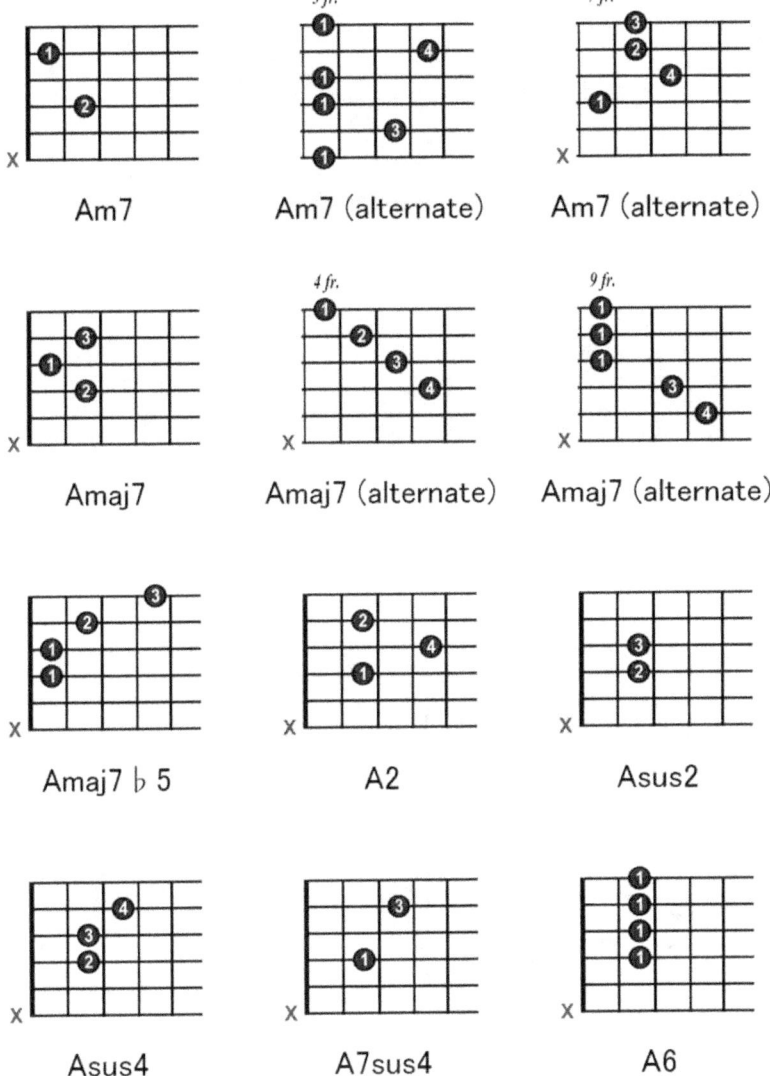

A

Am7 Am7 (alternate) Am7 (alternate)

Amaj7 Amaj7 (alternate) Amaj7 (alternate)

Amaj7 ♭ 5 A2 Asus2

Asus4 A7sus4 A6

A Chords

Continued

Am6

A9

Am9

Amaj9

Aadd9

Aadd9(no3)

A6/9

A7+9

A6/9

A7+9

A7−9

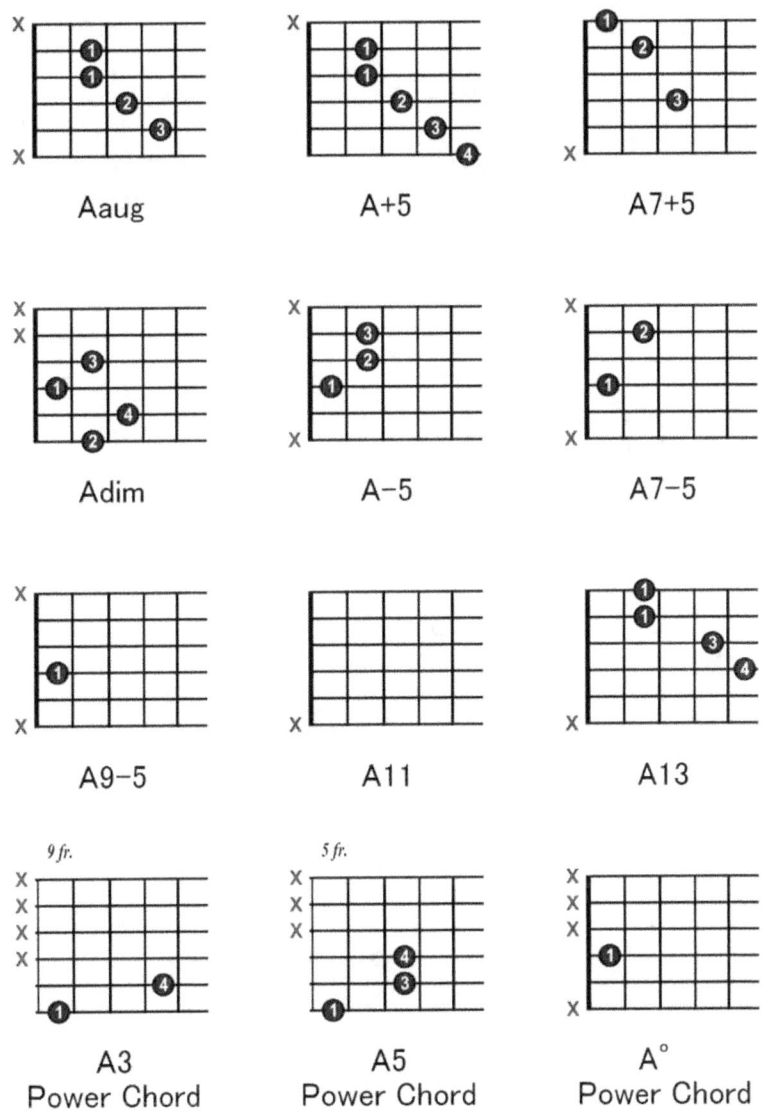

Aaug

A+5

A7+5

Adim

A−5

A7−5

A9−5

A11

A13

9 fr.

A3
Power Chord

5 fr.

A5
Power Chord

A°
Power Chord

B♭ Chords

B♭ is also known as A#

B♭

6 fr.

B♭ (alternate)

10 fr.

B♭ (alternate)

B♭7

6 fr.

B♭7 (alternate)

7 fr.

B♭7 (alternate)

B♭m

6 fr.

B♭m (alternate)

8 fr.

B♭m (alternate)

Big Guitar Chord Book
©2011 Moran Education http://www.MoranEducation.com/6Strings

B♭

B♭m7　　　B♭m7 (alternate)　　B♭m7 (alternate)

B♭maj7　　B♭maj7 (alternate)　B♭maj7 (alternate)

B♭maj7♭5　　　　B♭2　　　　　B♭sus2

B♭sus4　　　　B♭7sus4　　　　B♭6

B♭

Continued

Chords

B♭ m6

B♭ 9

4 fr.

B♭ m9

B♭ maj9

6 fr.

B♭ add9

B♭ add9(no3)

B♭ 6/9

B♭ 7+9

B♭ 7-9

B♭

B♭

B♭ aug

B♭ +5

B♭ 7+5

B♭ dim

B♭ −5

B♭ 7−5

B♭ 9−5

B♭ 11

B♭ 13

B♭ 3
Power Chord

B♭ 5
Power Chord

B♭ °
Power Chord

B

Chords

B

7 fr.

B (alternate)

9 fr.

B (alternate)

B7

2 fr.

B7 (alternate)

7 fr.

B7 (alternate)

Bm

7 fr.

Bm (alternate)

9 fr.

Bm (alternate)

B

Bm7 Bm7 (alternate) Bm7 (alternate)

Bmaj7 Bmaj7 (alternate) Bmaj7 (alternate)

Bmaj7 ♭ 5 B2 Bsus2

Bsus4 B7sus4 B6

B

Chosen

B
Chords

Continued

Bm6

B9

Bm9

Bmaj9

Badd9

Badd9(no3)

B6/9

B7+9

B7−9

B

Baug

B+5

B7+5

Bdim

B−5

B7−5

B9−5

B11

B13

B3
Power Chord

B5
Power Chord

B°
Power Chord

C
Chords

C

3 fr.

C (alternate)

8 fr.

C (alternate)

C7

3 fr.

C7 (alternate)

8 fr.

C7 (alternate)

Cm

3 fr.

Cm (alternate)

8 fr.

Cm (alternate)

©2011 Moran Education http://www.MoranEducation.com/6Strings

C

Cm7

Cm7 (alternate) 3 fr.

Cm7 (alternate) 8 fr.

Cmaj7

Cmaj7 (alternate) 3 fr.

Cmaj7 (alternate) 7 fr.

Cmaj7 ♭ 5

C2

Csus2

Csus4

C7sus4

C6

C

Chords

Continued

Cm6 C9 Cm9

Cmaj9 Cadd9 Cadd9(no3)

C6/9 C7+9 C7−9

Big Guitar Chord Book
©2011 Moran Education http://www.MoranEducation.com/6Strings

C

Caug

C+5

C7+5

Cdim

C−5

C7−5

C9−5

C11

C13

C3
Power Chord

8 fr.

C5
Power Chord

C°
Power Chord

C#

C# is also known as D♭

Chords

C#

C# (alternate)

C# (alternate)

C#7

C#7 (alternate)

C#7 (alternate)

C#m

C#m (alternate)

C#m (alternate)

C#

C#m7

C#m7 (alternate)

C#m7 (alternate)

C#maj7

C#maj7 (alternate)

C#maj7 (alternate)

C#maj7 ♭ 5

C#2

C#sus2

C#sus4

C#7sus4

C#6

C# | *Continued*

Chords

C#m6

C#9

C#m9

C#maj9

C#add9

C#add9(no3)

C#6/9

C#7+9

C#7−9

Big Guitar Chord Book
©2011 Moran Education http://www.MoranEducation.com/6Strings

C#aug

C#+5

C#7+5

C#dim

C#−5

C#7−5

C#9−5

C#11

C#13

C#3
Power Chord

C#5
Power Chord

C#°
Power Chord

D
Chords

D

D (alternate)

D (alternate)

D7

D7 (alternate)

D7 (alternate)

Dm

Dm (alternate)

Dm (alternate)

D

Dm7

Dm7 (alternate)

Dm7 (alternate)

Dmaj7

Dmaj7 (alternate)

Dmaj7 (alternate)

Dmaj7 ♭ 5

D2

Dsus2

Dsus4

D7sus4

D6

D

Chords

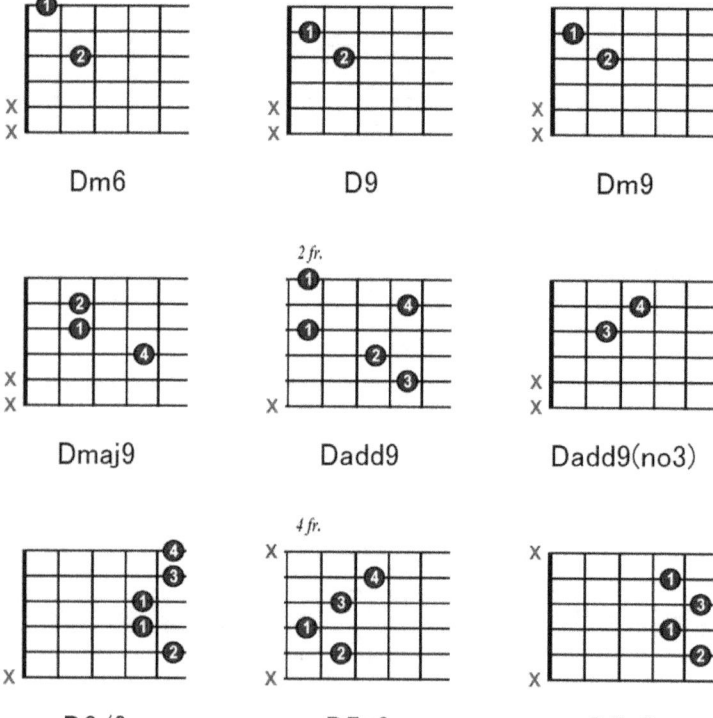

Dm6 D9 Dm9

2 fr.

Dmaj9 Dadd9 Dadd9(no3)

4 fr.

D6/9 D7+9 D7−9

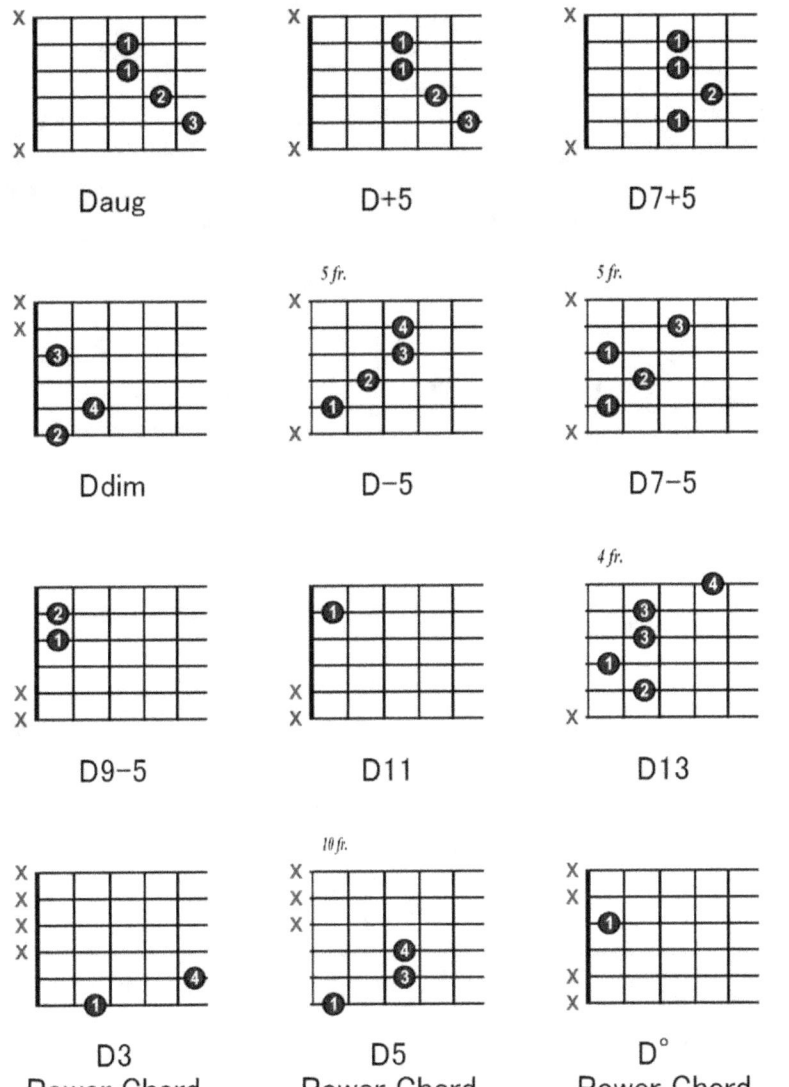

Daug

D+5

D7+5

Ddim

D−5

D7−5

D9−5

D11

D13

D3
Power Chord

D5
Power Chord

D°
Power Chord

E♭ Chords

E ♭ is also known as D#

E ♭

E ♭ (alternate)

E ♭ (alternate)

E ♭ 7

E ♭ 7 (alternate)

E ♭ 7 (alternate)

E ♭ m

E ♭ m (alternate)

E ♭ m (alternate)

E ♭

E♭

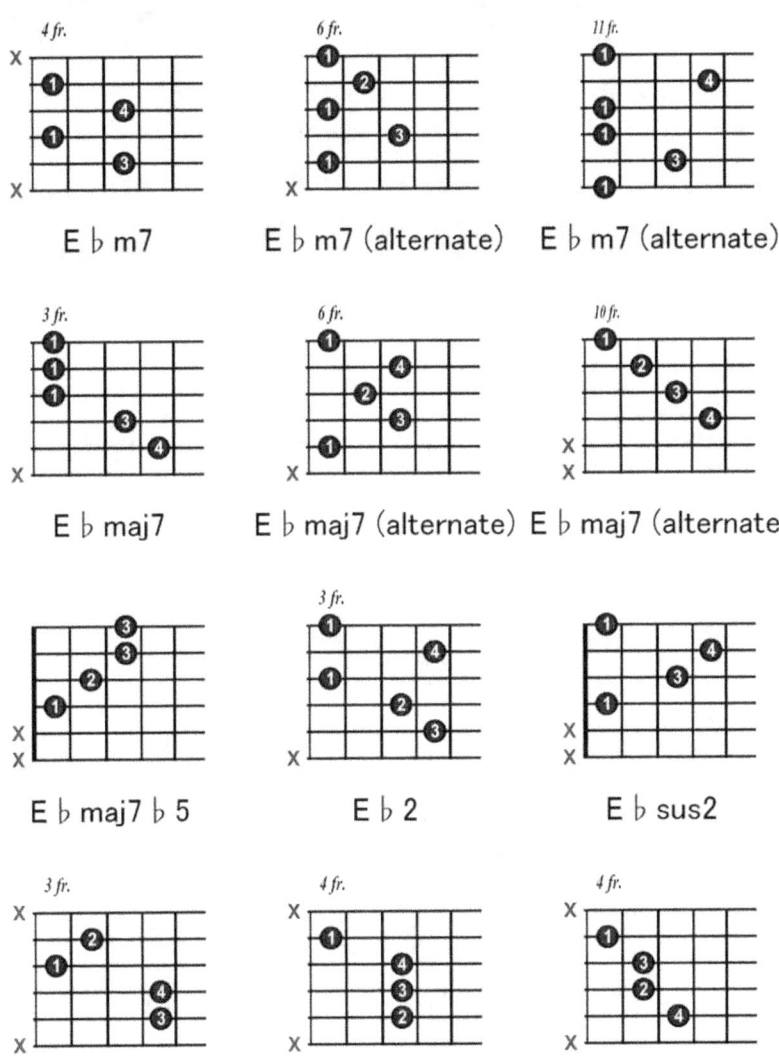

E♭ m7

E♭ m7 (alternate)

E♭ m7 (alternate)

E♭ maj7

E♭ maj7 (alternate)

E♭ maj7 (alternate)

E♭ maj7♭5

E♭ 2

E♭ sus2

E♭ sus4

E♭ 7sus4

E♭ 6

E♭ Chords

Continued

E♭ m6

E♭ 9

E♭ m9

E♭ maj9

E♭ add9

E♭ add9(no3)

E♭ 6/9

E♭ 7+9

E♭ 7−9

E♭

E♭ aug

E♭ +5

E♭ 7+5

E♭ dim

E♭ −5

E♭ 7−5

E♭ 9−5

E♭ 11

E♭ 13

E♭ 3
Power Chord

E♭ 5
Power Chord

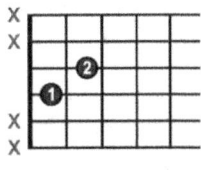

E♭ °
Power Chord

Big Guitar Chord Book

©2011 Moran Education http://www.MoranEducation.com/6Strings

E♭

E

Chords

E

E (alternate)

E (alternate)

E7

E7 (alternate)

E7 (alternate)

Em

Em (alternate)

Em (alternate)

E

Em7

Em7 (alternate) *3 fr.*

Em7 (alternate) *7 fr.*

Emaj7

Emaj7 (alternate) *4 fr.*

Emaj7 (alternate) *7 fr.*

Emaj7 ♭ 5

E2

Esus2

Esus4

E7sus4

E6

E

Chords

Em6

E9

Em9

Emaj9

Eadd9

Eadd9(no3)

E6/9

E7+9

E7−9

Eaug

E+5

E7+5

Edim

E-5

E7-5

E9-5

E11

E13

4 fr.

E3
Power Chord

E5
Power Chord

E°
Power Chord

F

Chords

F

F (alternate)
5 fr.

F (alternate)
8 fr.

F7

F7 (alternate)
6 fr.

F7 (alternate)
8 fr.

Fm

Fm (alternate)
3 fr.

Fm (alternate)
8 fr.

Big Guitar Chord Book
©2011 Moran Education http://www.MoranEducation.com/6Strings

Fm7

Fm7 (alternate)

Fm7 (alternate)

Fmaj7

Fmaj7 (alternate)

Fmaj7 (alternate)

Fmaj7 ♭ 5

F2

Fsus2

Fsus4

F7sus4

F6

F

Chords

Fm6

F9

Fm9

Fmaj9

Fadd9

3 fr.

Fadd9(no3)

F6/9

F7+9

F7-9

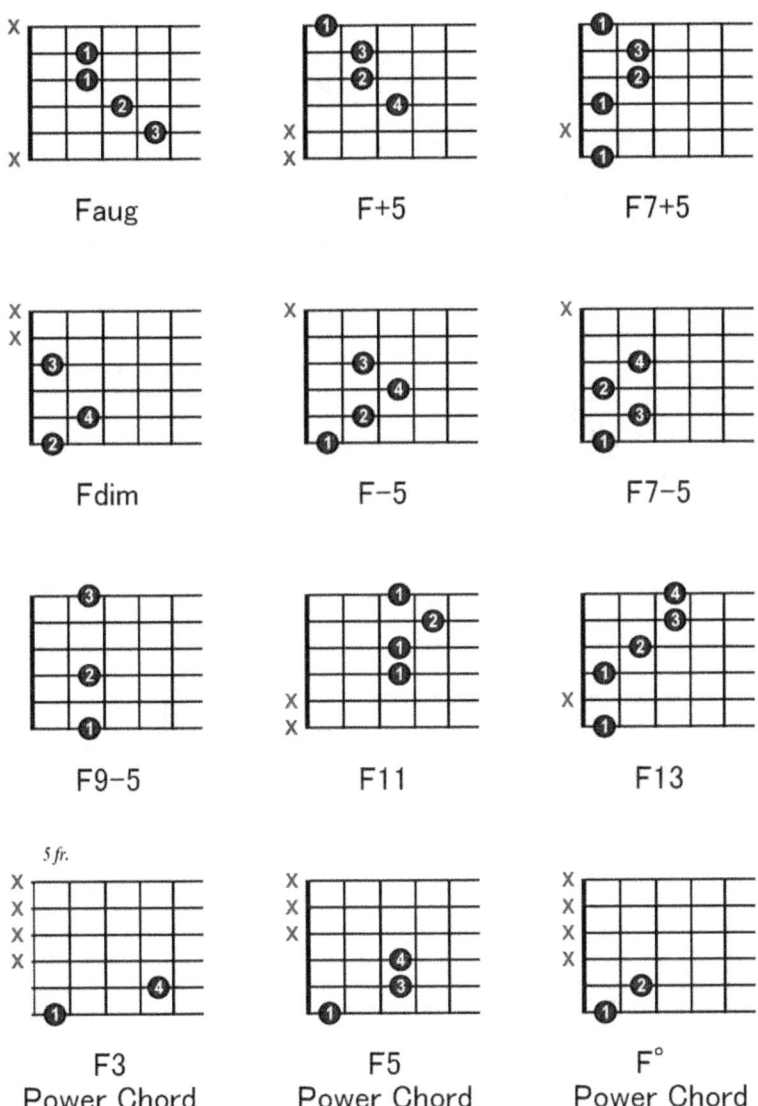

Faug

F+5

F7+5

Fdim

F−5

F7−5

F9−5

F11

F13

F3
Power Chord

F5
Power Chord

F°
Power Chord

F#

F# is also
known as G♭

Chords

F#

6 fr.

F# (alternate)

9 fr.

F# (alternate)

F#7

7 fr.

F#7 (alternate)

9 fr.

F#7 (alternate)

F#m

4 fr.

F#m (alternate)

9 fr.

F#m (alternate)

Big Guitar Chord Book

©2011 Moran Education http://www.MoranEducation.com/6Strings

F#m7

F#m7 (alternate)

F#m7 (alternate)

F#maj7

F#maj7 (alternate)

F#maj7 (alternate)

F#maj7 ♭ 5

F#2

F#sus2

F#sus4

F#7sus4

F#6

F#

Chords

F#m6

F#9

F#m9

F#maj9

2 fr.
F#add9

4 fr.
F#add9(no3)

F#6/9

F#7+9

F#7-9

F#

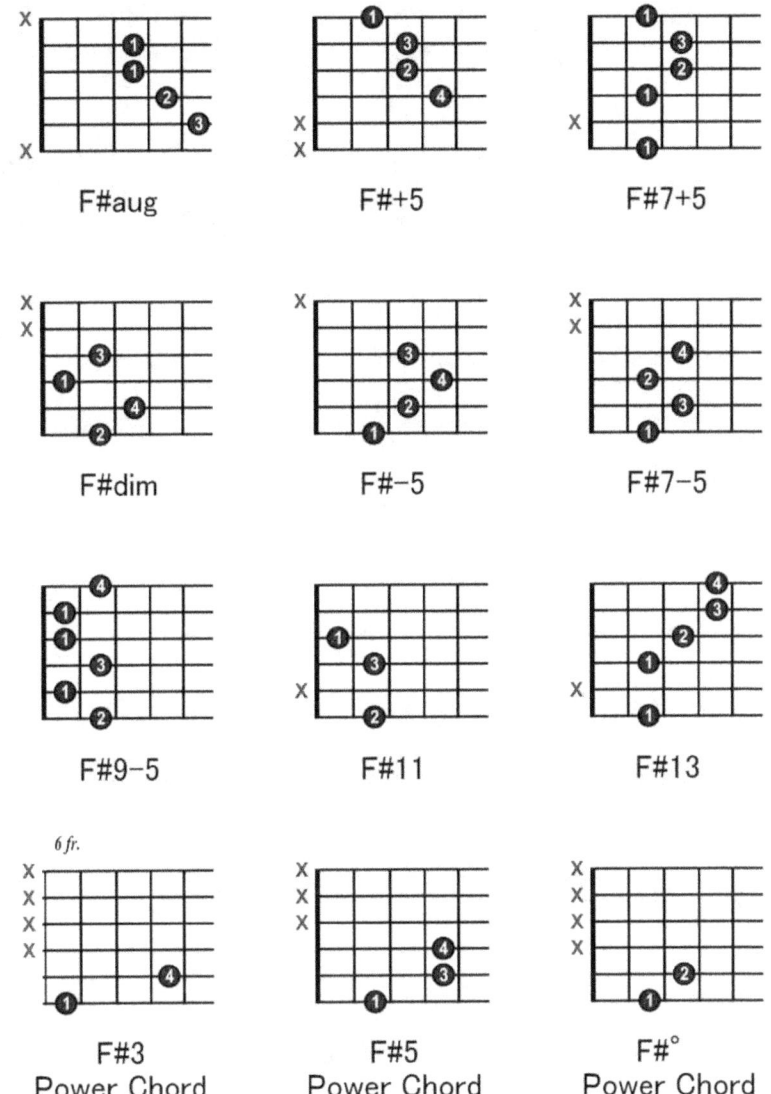

F#aug

F#+5

F#7+5

F#dim

F#−5

F#7−5

F#9−5

F#11

F#13

6 fr.

F#3
Power Chord

F#5
Power Chord

F#°
Power Chord

G

Chords

G

G (alternate)

3 fr.

G (alternate)

7 fr.

G7

G7 (alternate)

3 fr.

G7 (alternate)

8 fr.

Gm

Gm (alternate)

5 fr.

Gm (alternate)

10 fr.

Gm7   Gm7 (alternate)   Gm7 (alternate)

Gmaj7   Gmaj7 (alternate)   Gmaj7 (alternate)

Gmaj7 ♭5   G2   Gsus2

Gsus4   G7sus4   G6

G

Chords

Continued

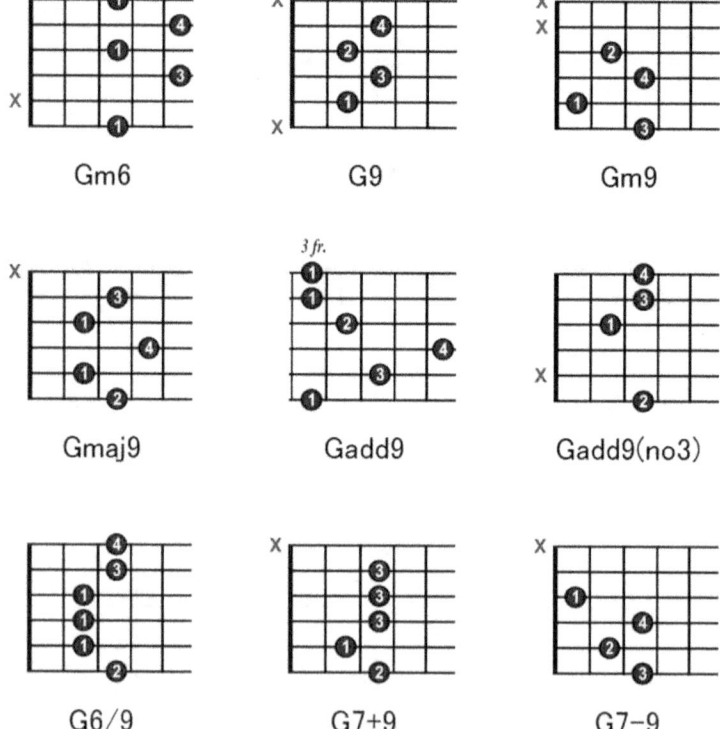

Gm6	G9	Gm9
Gmaj9	Gadd9	Gadd9(no3)
G6/9	G7+9	G7−9

Big Guitar Chord Book

©2011 Moran Education http://www.MoranEducation.com/6Strings

Gaug

G+5

G7+5

Gdim

G−5

G7−5

G9−5

G11

G13

7 fr.

G3
Power Chord

G5
Power Chord

G°
Power Chord

Index

Find Stuff

Section	Page No.
Introduction	2
A ♭ Chords	6
A Chords	10
B ♭ Chords	14
B Chords	18
C Chords	22
C# Chords	26
D Chords	30
E ♭ Chords	34
E Chords	38
F Chords	42
F# Chords	46
G Chords	50

6 Strings - Big Guitar Chord Book

Edition I

www.MoranEducation.com/6Strings

ISBN 978-1-4709-2711-0